THE
TARTAN-SPOTTER'S
GUIDE

by James D. Scarlett

'For Meta'

 VAN NOSTRAND REINHOLD COMPANY

NEW YORK   CINCINNATI   TORONTO   LONDON   MELBOURNE

Text and tartan patterns copyright © 1973 by James D. Scarlett
Illustrations copyright © 1973 by Angus McBride
Library of Congress Catalog Card Number: 76-15805
ISBN 0-442-27367-3

Printed in the United States of America.

Published in 1976 by Van Nostrand Reinhold Company
A division of Litton Educational Publishing, Inc.
450 West 33rd Street, New York, NY 10001

Van Nostrand Reinhold Limited
1410 Birchmount Road, Scarborough, Ontario M1P 2E7, Canada

16 15 14 13 12 11 10 9 8 7 6 5 4 3 2 1

Library of Congress Cataloging in Publication Data
Scarlett, James Desmond.
  The tartan-spotter's guide.

  Includes index.
  1. Tartans.   I. McBride, Angus.   II. Title.
DA880.H76S37 1976   929'.2'0941   76-15805
ISBN 0-442-27367-3

CONTENTS

PREFACE

At first, the idea of a book about tartans in which many of the illustrations are in monochrome may be a trifle disturbing (if not actually alarming) but in fact, in all matters pertaining to the study of tartan, it is the pattern that is important and colour is secondary to it.

Furthermore, the majority of tartan patterns — which are technically known as 'setts' — fall into one or other of a comparatively few simple types of pattern, so that when we have mastered the art of reducing a sett to its 'black and white' basis we can see it more clearly and relate it to other apparently different setts of the same family.

Starting with the simple designs, it becomes easy to create a framework upon which can be hung an almost complete identification system, by reference to which almost any tartan likely to be seen out and about can be identified readily, if not precisely 'at a glance'.

In any system such as this, there must be some 'rogue' patterns that do not fit the framework, and for the moment we must pass these by, but for the rest, reference to the tables included in the large section on Tartan Patterns (page 26) enables a tartan first to be 'typed' and then to be examined in detail to give an exact identification, so that it will no longer be necessary to identify every red tartan as Royal Stuart and every dark one as Black Watch. By using the Tartan Index on page 75, the process can be put into reverse, so that when the name of a tartan is known it can be described and drawn from the information given in the tables. A word of warning is needed here, though, for some names will appear under several tartans and it will often occur that some of those tartans, included here for the sake of completeness, are rarely if ever worn.

If success in dealing with the subject in this way is to be achieved, one cannot afford to be pedantic. The purist will argue that the stripes are woven into a tartan, but it is usually more convenient to describe them as superimposed on a ground colour; similarly, although patterns of the same group may be made up from elements which differ in detail from one sett to another, this will be found not to prejudice the argument or to affect the issue, which is to give a general idea of what a tartan looks like.

There are some groups of tartans whose dominant feature is, for most members of the group, some particular arrangement of some particular colours and these provide exceptions to the rule of thinking of tartan in monochrome. One example of such a group is the blue, black and green check that forms the basis of so many of the dark tartans, but there are some others, as we shall find.

By looking more carefully at tartan, we shall learn to see past superficial differences to real similarities and thence to the fringe of a fascinating study which goes much further than just recognising the patterns. This book sets out to provide the basis of that study in a light-hearted yet none the less factual manner. It is necessarily elementary, but then the beginning is always the best place to start.

INTRODUCTION

The available evidence will not sustain the notion that when Noah's Ark made its first landfall on Ben Nevis the first Highlander to disembark was wearing a Clan tartan that has come down to us unaltered. Indeed, an overwhelming part of it points in the opposite direction; at the very beginning of the eighteenth century Clansmen had to be ordered to turn out in uniform tartans, and in the plentiful selection of portraits of Highland Chiefs dating from between the two major Jacobite Risings of 1715 and 1745 there is no case in which the sitter is portrayed in anything resembling his modern Clan tartan. On the other side of the coin there are two well-known paintings of henchmen of one Chief in which the models are shown wearing very similar, but not quite identical tartans; a poem in Latin about the campaigns of Viscount Dundee which refers very clearly to the various regiments being in uniform; and a late seventeenth century book which states that a man's place of residence can be guessed from a sight of his plaid, which remark has been taken to mean that a completely regimented system of District tartans existed at that date.

8

While there is evidence to show that people had started to think of tartans in connection with Clans in the early years of the nineteenth century, there is even more to indicate that a man wore the pattern of tartan that he liked. What gave real and lasting impetus to the idea of every Clan having its tartan was the visit to Edinburgh by King George IV in 1822. From this time on, and particularly during the Victorian period, the Clan Tartan Idea got an ever-firmer grip and surrounded tartan with myths and fairy tales that have gradually become accepted as facts, except by a few inquiring minds.

A keynote of life in the Highlands of old was self-sufficiency. Trade was carried on, but the general rule was that the people of each community grew their own food, reared or hunted their own meat and built their own houses. The fine woollen cloth that they called 'tartan' was made from yarn spun by the women, coloured with dyes produced from local plants and woven by the local weaver. It is not likely that this weaver, endowed as he was with a captive circle of customers, would bother to make a wide range of patterns (if he made a range at all) and so a condition of 'one village, one tartan' could easily grow up. But the Highlander's choice of tartan would have been forced by availability, for the deliberate idea of 'one Clan, one tartan and one tartan, one Clan' had not then come about. However, because it was also generally true to say 'one village, one Clan' (or at any rate, one Clan and its adherents), it is not difficult to see a reason for the beginning of the Clan Tartan Idea.

Of recent years there has been a growing tendency to look on tartan in a more factual way but, although one may choose a tartan according to one's fancy, one is well advised to bear in mind that the Clan Tartan Idea is well enough established for it to be considered bad manners (or worse!) to lay claim to and wear a Clan tartan for empty reasons. There is a plentiful supply of what we may call universal tartans, from which the untartaned may choose, and thus there is no need to cause offence by wearing the tartan of a clan with which one has no real connection.

WHAT IS TARTAN?

In olden times, the word 'Tartan', said to have come originally from the French, was used to describe a particular kind of cloth, without any reference to its pattern. Although it is very likely that the type of pattern became associated with the name at an early date, there are signs that the word was usable in the old sense as late as the first quarter of the nineteenth century. This kind of tartan was a thin, hard material made from wool spun very fine and woven at as many as seventy threads to the inch; its texture was more like linen than a modern woollen cloth. Although made predominantly of wool, it was not uncommon, at least in later days, for some of the finer lines, the whites, yellows and sometimes the reds, to be put in with silk, which gave clearer colours and an enriched appearance.

This old 'hard' tartan was extremely durable and nearly weatherproof, but the advent of a softer life in the Highlands brought with it a demand for softer tartans.

The early textile industry produced these by weaving a soft-spun yarn on a hard-spun warp; the warp, which is the lengthwise thread of the cloth, takes the strain of weaving and so needs to be strong, while the weft, which runs back and forth across the cloth, need be no stronger than is necessary to hold it together. The soft tartan made in this way was

'... the same in both directions of the cloth'

called 'Rock and Wheel' from the warp yarn being spun with a 'rock' or distaff and spindle and the softer weft yarn with the spinning wheel.

It has always been customary for the pattern of tartan to be made the same in both directions of the cloth and for it to be made to repeat in reverse about regular pivotal lines, so that each section of the pattern is the mirror image of those immediately preceding and following it. But these rules are not unshakeable, and it is not difficult to find tartans in which the warp pattern differs from that of the weft, or others in which the pattern joins end to end without reversing. The latter are mainly of two kinds, modern aberrations that have come about because of some error in pattern taking, and sets that would be regular but for the presence of an overcheck in alternating colours. Nevertheless there are also a few old sets which repeat without the reverse.

12

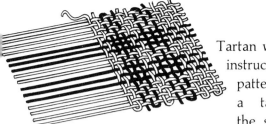

Tartan weavers note the instructions for each pattern in the form of a table in which the stripes are listed in order and the number of threads and the colour of each given; the warp, that is the whole bundle of warp threads needed to fill the required width of material, is made up in accordance with this table and loaded on to the loom, and the weft is then woven across it. On the loom the warp will appear as a series of stripes running fore and aft, and will not take on the appearance of a tartan until the weft is put in.

The word 'Tartan' nowadays means both the pattern and the cloth; the whole product can be described as a cloth woven from coloured yarns in a pattern of lines and stripes which repeats regularly throughout the length and the width. In wool, tartan may be made 'hard' (though not so hard as formerly) by using a worsted yarn, or 'soft' using a tweed or saxony yarn. There is a modern equivalent to Rock and Wheel, though not advertised as such, in which a saxony weft is woven on a worsted warp. Tartan is also commonly made in silk and cotton and, of course, in the man-made fibres, but whatever the material, the essence of it is that the pattern is woven in, not printed on.

The matter of a tartan pattern being made up of inter-woven stripes put together in a regular arrangement that repeats end-over-end along and across the cloth is of great importance to us, for it puts in our hands a simple and compact method of notation.

Its essence lies in the fact that, in the great majority of cases, the pattern of stripes is the same in both directions of the cloth. Because of this we can, in our mind's eye, dispense with the chequer pattern of the full tartan and look instead at the stripes only of the warp set up in the loom. We can draw this, setting out the bands of colour in accordance with the proportions given by the thread count and filling in the colours with poster colour or felt-tipped pen, to make what is termed a colour strip, a strip rather like a medal ribbon that shows all we need to know about the pattern. We shall have more to say about the "professional" way of dealing with these colour strips later; for the present it will be evident that they can be drawn on cards or put away in a loose-leaf book, accompanied in each case by any information, such as the thread-count and source of the pattern, that may be relevant.

Tackled in this way, a tartan collection will soon take shape, without the need to weave specimens or to beg them from some dealer in tartans.

To help to get your eye in, each tartan illustration in the book has its shaded 'colour' strip alongside and full-colour strips for more than

thirty tartans are given at the end. These have a dual purpose and, apart from just being colour-strips, permit us to illustrate some of the more complicated tartans.

We have also included thread-counts for a couple of dozen sets and these also have a dual purpose; they are there to provide material for those who want to have a shot at drawing colour strips and, since at the time of writing there is very little in the way of source-material for the tartan weaver, it is hoped that they will be of use to anyone who has aspirations in this direction. This is, however, no place for a treatise on the art of weaving. For that you must go elsewhere, and glance at the section entitled "Further Reading".

HOW IT ALL BEGAN

From the earliest times for which we have records, that is to say from the time of the Roman occupation of these islands, reports have come down telling of the Celtic peoples rejoicing in bright colours and wearing 'cloaks' that were 'striped', 'variegated', 'marled' and so on. In those days there was no word for tartan as we know it, and such descriptions would have been the nearest that the casual observer would be likely to get to it, but this does not mean (as it is too easy for our own wishful thoughts to tell us) that every time someone said 'striped', he meant 'tartan'.

Tartan weaving is simple weaving and tartan produces an exuberant effect by the use of colour in small areas. This has much to recommend it when the dyeing is done in a two-gallon pot over a peat fire, as was the case in former days, so it is by no means unlikely that the Celts and the Picts used tartan patterns. But their probable use is no ground for assuming that Hadrian's Wall was ever assaulted by Highland regiments drawn up in Clan order and wearing Clan tartans.

The first clear mention of tartan in an historical document occurs in 1538, when the Lord High Treasurer

purchased three ells
of 'Helande Tertane'
for the making of
trews for King James V.
Again we must beware,
and take care to note that
tartan for a Stewart king does
not necessarily mean Royal
Stuart tartan. The chances are
that such a 'tertane' would be one
of the check patterns that remained
popular for trews over a long period.
An 'ell', by the way, is an old measure
of length; in Scotland it was equal to thirty-
seven English inches, but varied somewhat
elsewhere.

In 1578 John Leslie, Bishop of Ross, published his
'History of Scotland'. From this we can learn, thanks to a trans-
lation made in 1596, that all the Highlanders, nobility and
common people alike, wore 'mantles' of 'one form' (i.e. the

same kind), except that those of the nobility were larger and of more and brighter colours. From this it has been inferred that the number of colours in a man's plaid were a mark of his rank, but the truth is that it was the same then as it is today, and the man who could afford it could have what he wanted while the man who could not had to put up with buying his clothes 'off the peg'.

As the years pass, mentions of tartan in historical records become more frequent, but still without giving us any details of what it looked like. It is, for example, recorded that tartan was included among the manufactures of Scottish colonists of Ulster at the end of the sixteenth century, and in 1607 'Camden's Britannia' again gives a reference to the 'striped mantles' of the Highlanders. A series of Crown Charters, dated from 1587 to 1630 and concerning the lands of Norraboll in Islay, set the annual feu duty at 'sixty ells of cloth in colour white, black, and green' but in spite of the best efforts of researchers it has not been possible to prove with any degree of conclusiveness that this was tartan cloth.

An important, frequently printed but seldom quoted, piece of evidence occurs in the form of a German broadsheet of 1631 which depicts four Highland soldiers, generally believed to be members of MacKay's Regiment that served under Gustavus Adolphus. The various forms of dress shown need not concern us greatly at this point, but almost for the first time, these drawings show a recognisably tartan pattern. Incidentally, one of the figures shows a much better delineation of the belted plaid than many, more modern, artists have managed to produce.

The next important reference comes in Martin Martin's 'Description of the Western Isles', published in 1703. Writing of the pattern of the plaid, Martin tells us that

'Every Isle differs from each other in their Fancy of making Plads, as to the Stripes in Breadth and Colours. This Humour is as different thro the main Land of the Highlands, in-so-far that they who have seen those places, are able at the first View of a Man's Plad, to guess the Place of his Residence...'

This passage has been taken as evidence of the existence of a well-ordered system of District Tartans in Martin's time, but the only solid implication behind it is that local types of pattern existed, and this would not have been surprising in a country of small communities, each with its own weaver making his own patterns or, very likely, just one single pattern.

While one or two pieces of cloth survived from the period of the 1715 Rising until recent—if not present—times, it is mainly to portraits that we have to turn for information about tartan patterns of the first half of the eighteenth century. Particular among these is the fine collection of paintings of Grant Chiefs and their retainers, owned by the Seafield Trust and chiefly remarkable because none of the Chiefs is shown in any Grant tartan now known. Nor are

any two of the tartans shown the same; even the tartans of the Champion and the Piper, though similar, are not quite identical. Although we should not of course expect photographic accuracy from a painter, it is a little strange that such great disparities should exist. And this is especially so in the case of Grant portraits, for it was the Laird of Grant who on two separate occasions, in 1703 and 1705, ordered his men to turn out for hunting matches in uniform tartans. So we might expect that the Grants, of all the Clans, would have been aware of the idea of uniform Clan tartans. The portraits indicate otherwise.

With the failure of the Jacobite Rising of 1745 came many harsh measures aimed at destroying the Clans and the power of their Chiefs, among them the forbidding of tartan and Highland dress to all except Highland soldiers of the British Army. In the end, oppression and brutality probably ensured the survival of tartans and Highland dress, both of which might have disappeared completely had the ordinary forces of 'civilization' been employed in the Highlands. But during the period of the proscription, which lasted the thirty-five years from 1747 to 1782, much was lost to us. For tartan ceased to be a local product and became concentrated in the Lowlands, and the few fragments of tartan that survived from before that time are almost all in some way associated with the Rising and consequently cannot be regarded as typical examples.

MODERN TIMES

When the Dress Act was repealed in 1782, there was little left of Highland Tartan but a vague memory of distinctive Clan tartans and a thriving Lowland weaving industry making tartan for military use and export. On the former, General David Stewart of Garth and Alexander Robertson of Struan were corresponding in 1815 concerning the desirability of preserving examples of the old Clan tartans; the difficulties of which may be judged from a passage in one of Struan's letters which reads as follows:

> 'More than twenty years ago I wished to ascertain what the pattern of the Clandonachy (i.e. Robertson) Tartan was, and applied to different old men of the Clan for information, most of whom pretended to know what the pattern was, but as no two of the descriptions I received were exactly similar, and as they were all very vulgar and gaudy, I did not think proper to adopt any of them.'

Struan adds that, as he had then worn the tartan commonly called the Athol Tartan for nearly thirty years, he proposed to continue to do so. But a Robertson tartan was featured in a manufacturer's pattern list of 1819, and what was then listed as 'Athol tartan' is now Murray of Athol.

Happily, the Lowland weaving industry provides us with many more facts. The firm of William Wilson & Son came into existence at Bannockburn, probably at about the middle of the eighteenth century — the earliest known account books are dated 1765 and there was a family tradition that it had begun weaving in the days of William's father, about 1724 — and remained a going concern until 1924, although it was reconstituted in 1907, when it changed its line of business from tartan weaving to carpet weaving.

Wilson's grew so big, and so much in the way of their records has survived, that there is constant danger to the student that he will fall into the trap of thinking of them as being the only tartan weavers of the day, and not just the biggest. We are fortunate not only that Wilson's preserved so much in the way of written records, but also that when the Company wound up these passed into the hands of people who had an interest in their further preservation. The result is that, stored away in such places as the National Library of Scotland, the National Museum of the Antiquities of Scotland, and in the collections of the Scottish Tartans Society, a wealth of information awaits detailed study, a wealth that can only be judged from the value of the small part that has already been examined. In these letters and other papers we can read the weaving patterns and instructions recorded for the firm's own use in 1819 and handle pieces of cloth, some made before 1800, that are attached to orders sent in from as far away as Exeter. Letters concerning a man who wanted a suit in the Royal Stuart tartan; one from a North of England customer who sent a specimen of red and green check and asked for a piece of this pattern 'but without the red'; and an order from a canny Irishman who sent with it thirty halves of £1 notes, saying that Wilson's could have the other halves if the goods were up to scratch. All these help to bring their writers to life before us and to reveal much about the business

... thirty halves of

methods of the day. Some of the letters are elegantly written models of what a business letter should be, some appear to be painstaking compositions in English from men whose mother-tongue was Gaelic, and yet another tells us of a chance missed when a customer enquired if there were such a thing as a Flowers of Edinburgh tartan; tantalizingly, there is no reply attached, but then there is no Flowers of Edinburgh tartan either. In modern times, such a question would have been answered much more efficiently, if we can believe the story of the Brown Watch tartan, according to which a North American merch̬ ordered from Scotland a quantity of Black Watch, adding as an afterthought 'please send one bale of Brown Watch'. The order was promptly fulfilled, without comment or demur. The customer is always right!

Through the Wilson records much of the growth of the Clan Tartan System can be followed, from the small but

£1 notes . . .

increasing numbers of named tartans listed in the first two decades of the nineteenth century, through the great flood released upon the occasion of the visit of King George IV to Edinburgh in 1822, when many tartans that had hitherto been only numbers in a pattern book were adopted as Clan tartans, and Highland dress again became fit for a king (even if a trifle unsuitable for that one!): then on into the steady flow of Victorian times when, its dignity sealed by Royal approval, tartan climbed to the peak of popularity and Highland dress became the epitome of fancy dress.

In the years between, as manufacturing processes improved, heavier and hairier cloths came along and the old natural dyestuffs were replaced by synthetic ones, the bright but gentle colours of the old setts became vivid and harsh until, at about the end of the first World War, somebody had the ingenious idea of inventing 'Ancient' colours. These were certainly much more like the colours produced by the old methods of dyeing although some of the subtleties of the old colouring were lost in the transition. More recently still, another range of colours has made its appearance. These are called 'Reproduction' colours, and are based on the colours of a piece of tartan dug up on Culloden Moor in 1946. Tartan is a live business. It was developing two hundred years ago and there is no reason to regret that it should be doing so to-day, but it is a bit confusing to the beginner to be confronted with so many colours whose names carry the implication that the tartan is of great age. We can only refer again to our guiding principle, that it is the sett of a tartan that matters; the colours are to the customer's choice.

Although there is still a tendency among some Highland outfitters to the opinion that anyone who wants to wear Highland dress is an eccentric millionaire, the kilt is now beginning to show signs of a revival for general wear. Often enough, in the Highlands it will be seen on a visitor and will have an unfortunate reach-me-down appearance, but there are some who wear it for comfort and suitability and some visitors who wear it when they get back home.

John Taylor, the Water Poet, wrote of the Highlanders in 1618 ". . . if men be kind unto them, and be in their habit; then they are conquered with kindness, and the sport will be plentiful." This sentiment is as true to-day as it was the day it was written.

TARTAN PATTERNS

Plain Checks

The probable origin of all tartans is to be found in a pattern that few people will regard as a tartan at all — the Shepherd plaid. This small check design is all that is required of a tartan; it is of wool, woven in self-coloured, undyed

threads in the twill weave that is traditional for tartan and responsible for the distinctive diagonal ribbing of the cloth. And it has a regularly repeating pattern that is the same in both directions of the cloth. To call such a neat and well planned pattern 'primitive' may seem unfair, yet the traditional use of naturally-coloured fleeces for the yarn used in weaving the plaid shows it to have been the product of people who did not know how, or else could not be bothered, to dye their textiles.

The colour contrast between even the dark brown and cream shades of the naturally-coloured wool is considerable, and the size of the check can be increased only a very little before the result becomes unacceptably 'loud'. Consequently, the next step towards the development of a true tartan had to wait for colour to arrive.

With colour, much larger checks could be made and these were popular over a long period for trews. The only one of this simple group of patterns that is seen to-day is the black-and-red **Rob Roy,** but there was also a red-and-green version named **MacLauchlan** and one maker christened his black-and-green check pattern **'Robin Hood'.**

So simple a design, in so limited a colour range does not need an identification table, but is most useful in introducing the idea of strips and tables.

The 'colour strip' at the head of the table is a diagrammatic representation of the design in the warp threads, in which the various elements are differentiated by shading. Each column in the table represents an element, as indicated by the patch of shading at its head, so by reading across against each name we can relate name, colours and pattern. The colour symbols used are the standard ones listed on the back cover flap.

Plain Checks

Name		
MacGregor ('Rob Roy')	R	K
MacLauchlan	R	G
'Robin Hood'	G	K
Shepherd	W	K

Easy, isn't it? This idea is the one used for the description of the majority of patterns in the book. It remains simple, even though there are more elements in the 'colour strips' of the more complicated tartans. A complete understanding of the way this first table works will be of great help in making full use of those which follow.

Checks with Overchecks

The range of colours obtainable from the native dye-plants was severely limited and the range of suitable combinations even more so. The number of check patterns could thus never be more than a few, and other ways had to be found to increase the number of designs available.

One simple way of doing this is to add a fine line overcheck to each main check, thus breaking up the pattern and at the same time introducing accenting contrasts. The sketch below shows how each black check has now developed a frame of black 'dashes' around it and each white one a black point at its centre.

Again we show a 'colour strip' of the warp threads and this is used at the head of the identification table on page 31.

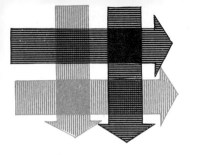

It is not always understood that, because the pattern is woven into the tartan, and not printed on, every colour is mixed in equal proportions with every other colour, thus producing many more colours in the printed cloth than went into it.

Nor is it always appreciated that no more than two colours can be mixed at a time and that no two unmixed colours can appear alongside each other, but must join point to point, on the diagonal.

There is actually a formula for working out the total number of colours, which the mathematically minded may care to try out: if N is the number of colours to start with, the number of colours plus blends in the finished cloth is given by $(N+1)\frac{N}{2}$, that is, the number of colours plus one is multiplied by half the number of colours. Thus, two colours finishes up as three, four as ten, and six, which is the normal maximum for the general run of setts, as twenty-one shades.

An overcheck can be a simple line, or it can have narrow edges of another colour, called 'guard lines'. Alternatively, it can be a group of lines, either separated with the ground showing between or running together to make a composite band. The colours of an overcheck frequently alternate in successive repeats of the design, and this is indicated in the tables by an oblique stroke between the colours, as R/Y; for composite lines, the colours are run together, as KYKYK and for multiple lines the number is given. Have a look at the **Cunningham, MacDonald of Kingsburgh** and **MacKinnon** patterns in the table on page 31 for examples.

Name	▒	▨	■	☐	Comments
Connel	R	K	W	Y	
Cunningham	R	K	2B, W in centre	2R	(1)
Ramsay	R	K	2C	2W	
Wallace	R	K	K	Y	
Bryce	R	G	Y	R	
Erskine	R	G	2G	2R	(1)
Lennox	R	LG	2C	2W	(2)
MacDonald of Kingsburgh	R	G	YGRGY	3Y	(3)
MacKinnon	R	G	K/W	R	
,, , Hunting	T	G	G/W	R	
Barclay, Hunting	B	G	G	R	
Douglas, green	B	G	W	K, A guards.	
Johnston	B	G	3K	2K, central Y	
Keith (Austin)	B	G	2K	K	(4)
Oliphant (Melville)	B	G	2K	2W	
Barclay, Dress	K	Y	Y	W	
MacLachlan	K	Y	2Y	2K	(1, 5)
MacRae of Conchra	B	W	Y	R	
Home	B	K	2G	2R near each edge	(1)
Douglas, grey	N	K	2K	2N near each edge	(1)

(1) See also the section entitled Counterchange patterns (page 32).
(2) Has also a C line at the junction of R and G.
(3) Has a white line at the junction of R and G.
(4) The two K lines are rather wide, and the effect is of a band of equal BKBKB construction.
(5) Has a yellow line near the edge of the black and, hence a black line at the edge of the yellow.

Counterchange Patterns

An important type of design, although one of which there are but a few examples, derives from the check-with-overcheck group. The principle of this design is that of counterchange, the pattern being composed of two parts, each of which is what may conveniently be called the negative image of the other.

Examples are **Erskine,** a red and green check, with a double red overcheck on green and a double green one on red, and **MacLachlan,** which has the same scheme but in black and yellow with the additional feature of a yellow line near the edge of the black and so a black line near the edge of the yellow. **Cunningham** departs somewhat from the

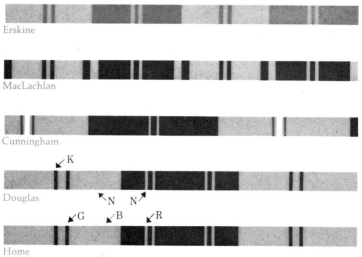

Erskine

MacLachlan

Cunningham

Douglas

Home

essential principle by taking a white line centred on the red element in addition to the double black that is part of the basic design, and the grey **Douglas,** while containing only two colours, changes its aspect slightly by putting a pair of grey lines near each edge of the black square, instead of having a single pair centrally upon the ground. The Douglases and the Homes are anciently connected, and the tartans underline the connection. The **Home** tartan changes the grey with black lines of **Douglas** to blue with green lines and has red lines in place of grey on the black.

Counterchange Pattern

All these tartans made their first appearance in a compendious volume entitled 'Vestiarium Scoticum' published in Edinburgh in 1842. We shall have more to say about this later. For the present, it is useful to try comparing the strips and visualizing the tartans. If real specimens of the cloth are available, so much the better.

Striped Patterns

Towards the end of the 1820's, when the Great Tartan Rush had got nicely under way, there appeared on the scene the brothers John and Charles Sobieski, variously known also as Hay, Hay-Allen and Sobieski-Stuart. They were widely believed to be legitimate grandsons of Prince Charles Edward and they claimed to have in their possession a manuscript dating from the end of the sixteenth century and giving details of ancient Clan tartans. Supposedly, this manuscript had been found in the library of the Scots College at Douai, and hence became known as the Douai Manuscript. The brothers claimed ownership of another edition, found at the St Augustine Monastery at Cadiz, and of a 'late and inferior copy', the Cromarty Manuscript. Only the last of these has ever been seen by eyes other than the brothers' own, and modern critical examination has left us little room to doubt that the whole thing was a forgery—and not even a very clever one. Quite apart from the question of authenticity, however, neither the Cromarty Manuscript nor the published version of the manuscripts, the 'Vestiarium Scoticum' (Vest. Scot.) which came out in 1842, give any precise details of the setts listed, so the published illustrations can only be the brothers' own interpretations of the descriptions.

At the time, however, few were inclined to quibble or to ask questions and the brothers made a great name for themselves, giving out the 'genuine original sett' of his Clan to any Chief who cared to ask.

Perhaps because of this, and the consequent strain on their powers of invention, most of the tartans illustrated in the Vestiarium show marked lack of originality, about half of them being nothing more than simple schemes of stripes grouped on a ground.

'. . . designed on a drawing board . . .'

Generally, the stripes are all of equal width and the whole group occupies about the same width as that of the exposed ground. Sometimes the stripes are of different colours, as in **Fraser,** where the outer stripes of the group of four are green and the inner ones blue, and sometimes the outer stripes may be of a different width, but the general effect is not very interesting and produces a result that appears to have been designed on a drawing board rather than on a loom.

Three-stripe patterns

Name					Comments
Hamilton*	R	B	B	W	(1)
MacGregor*	R	G	G	—	W, usually with K guards, on central G
Munro*	R	K	K	W	
Forbes*	G	K	K	R	Y on central K
Graham*	G	K	K	—	
Hamilton, Hunting	G	B	B	W	(1)
MacFarlane*	K	W	W	—	
Macleod	Y	K	K	R	
MacPherson, Dress*	W	K	K	2R	(2)
'Duchess of York'	T	G	K	B/W	

Tartans marked* are from Vest.Scot., but Macgregor was listed by Wilson's of Bannockburn in 1819 as 'MacGregor Murray Tartan'.
(1) Hamilton, Hunting, is a direct change of colour on the red tartan.
(2) Dress MacPherson is usually seen with a Y overcheck on the central band of K, but the tartan was re-recorded in 1948 with this line in white, as **'MacPherson of Cluny'.**

37

Four-stripe patterns

Name	▦	▨	▩	☐	Comments
Cameron, Hunting	B	G	G	GYG	R between G bars
Dollar Academy	B	K	K	W	
MacKay*	B	K	K	R	
MacQueen*	K	R	R	Y	(1)
Fraser, Hunting	T	G	B	R/W	
Buchanan*	W	C	C	K	
MacIntyre*	G	B	B	W	(2)
Gunn	G	K	B	R	
MacKay	G	K	B	K	
Morrison	G	K	B	K	G at centre, between B bars
Brodie, Dress*	R	K	K	K	(3)
Cameron, Clan*	R	G	G	Y	
Fraser*	R	G	B	W	
MacIan*	R	K	K	Y, K guards	(1)
Crawford*	C	G	G	2W	

As before, * denotes tartans that first appeared in Vest.Scot.
(1) **MacQueen** is a direct reversal of **MacIan,** which is spelt **MacKeane** in the original.
(2) The space between the outer blue bars is filled in with red.
(3) The four black bars are separated by three stripes, of which the outer two are yellow and the central one red.

The tartans that appeared in the Vestiarium had to be simple enough to be described without illustration by 'Sir Richard Urquhart, Knight', the reputed author of the Douai manuscript, but the tartan weavers, who were also

Name	▦	▨	▓	☐	Comments
Bruce*	R	G	G	W/Y	
Cumming* (MacAulay)	R	G	G	K	W line on wide G (1)
Maxwell*	R	K	G	2G	
Wemyss*	R	K	K	2G	W line on wide K
MacLean*	G	K	K	K	W line on wide K
Lauder*	G	K	B	R	(2)
Davidson	G	K	K	K	(3)
			alternate with		
		B	B		
Henderson	G	As	Davidson	—	Y between wide K, W between wide B

Once again, * indicates a tartan from Vest.Scot.
(1) There is another **Cumming** tartan, otherwise identical, with two narrow G bars instead of the single one.
(2) **Maitland,** the tartan of the Master of Lauderdale, has a composite overcheck of YBYRYBR instead of plain red.
(3) The thin central bar between the wide K/K and B/B stripes is always red.

the designers, suffered from no such hindrance, and so there are some stripe-based designs of considerable complexity to be found upon the tartan merchants' shelves.

We are a lot better off than was 'Sir Richard', for we have colour strips to help us to visualize the basic form, after which we need consider only the differences.

The whole series derives directly from Wilsons' **'Rae Tartan'** of 1819 (strip No 3, page 82), which becomes **MacRae** when a white line is added on each side of the paired blue bars, but thereafter the colours are changed and the tartan becomes a red one, of which **Ross** (strip No 4, page 82) is the simplest version. The red **MacRae** tartan adds a white line to **Ross** in the same way and place as the green, Wilsons', version added it to **Rae,** and **Huntly** (originally 'The Marchioness of Huntly's Tartan' and now used as a District sett) adds also a yellow line to the outside edge of the pairs of blue lines. Wilsons listed a tartan named **Kinnoul,** the same as the red **MacRae** derived from strip 4 but with the triple fine lines in black instead of blue, and

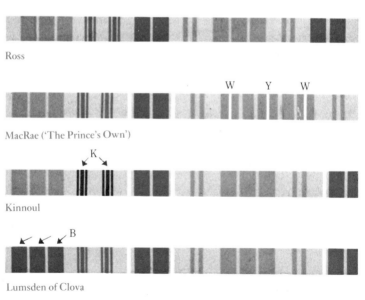

Ross

MacRae ('The Prince's Own')

Kinnoul

Lumsden of Clova

40

there is a **Lumsden of Clova** tartan, also the same as this red **MacRae,** but with alternate groups of three green bars in blue.

A popular method of varying this tartan still further has been to alter the arrangement of alternate green pivots, a change that can be shown simply and with best effect by means of shaded 'colour strips' on the opposite page.

The Mackintosh Group

We have already referred to certain groups of design in which a particular colour relationship is a dominant feature and the **Mackintosh** tartan now provides us with a good example of this class. This simple design of two broad green bands having a blue line between them and a narrow blue bar on each side of the pair, all upon a red ground, has been widely borrowed, and the Clan names associated with the designs so made suggest very strongly that it was quite common practice for a weaver to borrow from the man next door and add his own variations, in order to produce a 'new' design. This was then pirated by the next man down the line and so on. Through the whole series, the general layout remains very much the same, although the relative widths of

*'. . . common practice for a
weaver to borrow from
the man next door . . .'*

41

the stripes may vary and they may be moved closer together or further apart, (thus demonstrating another point already made, that general principles do not depend upon precise details).

Simple variants upon the theme are an early nine-teenth century **Chisholm** tartan, which takes a white line centrally upon each blue bar, a late nineteenth century and now almost forgotten **MacBean,** which had a black line centred on the red ground, and the modern **Shaw** tartan, designed within the past couple of years for the Chief, Shaw of Tordarroch, who wished to have a genuine tartan which would show his Clan's Mackintosh ancestry, in place of the entirely false tartan that had previously been sold under the name. This new and approved tartan for all Highland Shaws superimposes a light blue line with black guard lines upon the red ground of the Mackintosh tartan. Some other examples of the Mackintosh group are shown in colour strips 8, 9, 10, 11 and 12 on pages 82 and 83, but two are especially worthy of mention at this point.

A little knowledge (which is so dangerous a thing) led some years ago to a tartan then referred to as the **Childers Universal Tartan** being officially recommended for wear by the English and untartaned foreigners. In its very early days, the Scottish Tartans Society devoted considerable time to finding out how this came about and how the tartan originated. It soon became clear that the tartan is neither 'Childers' nor 'Universal', and it was eventually established that it was designed for the pipers of 1st Battalion, 1st Gurkha Rifles, but this is by the way. What is of present interest is that it is a dark green tartan directly based upon **Mackintosh** (the name of the designer of Childers Universal is given in some quarters as Mackintosh, which would account for this). To make the Gurkha tartan out of

Mackintosh, we first change red to black, and the blue stripes to what is described as Ash green; the ordinary green becomes Beech green and the central blue line red.

Hunting Stewart is another tartan that has suffered from some misunderstanding, but it is more than likely that this is due only to a spot of minor interference by the Sobieski brothers. Its interest for us lies partly in its being a truly universal tartan, suitable for general wear without any annoyance to anybody, but principally in that, in its earlier version, shown in strip 7 on page 82, the motif of the Mackintosh group, two wide stripes flanked by two narrow, can clearly be seen in two parts of the sett, in blue on black and in black on blue. The more modern version of this design, exhibiting double black lines on the blue section, seems most likely to have been brought about by the efforts of the Sobieski brothers to bring the design into line with the other Stewart tartans, most of which have this feature—the distinguishing feature of the Black Watch group.

Both **Mackintosh** and **Shaw** have their **Hunting** versions, made by changing the large area of red ground to green; Shaw keeps the light blue line and Mackintosh takes a yellow one centrally on this green ground.

44

Three-colour Checks

Probably the largest of all the design groups, although it falls neatly into several sections, is that of the three-colour check. This is another group that is strongly associated with a particular colour arrangement and usually, though not by any means invariably, consists of large squares of blue and green with black bars between.

In the simple form, almost all the setts have over-checks and some have a contrasting edge to one colour next the black. The MacDonald group is a subdivision of this type, as is the Black Watch, with its widely used motif and some interesting colour changes.

Three-colour checks

Name				||||	□	Comments
Baird	B	K	G	2K	3P	
Campbell of Loudoun	B	K	G	2K	W/Y, K guards	
Campbell of Cawdor	B	K	G	R, K guards	A, K guards	
Colquhoun	B	K	G	2K	R	W edge to G or B
Davidson of Tulloch	B	K	G	R	W	
Dundas*	B	K	G	K	K, 2R	
Ferguson of Atholl	B	K	G	—	W, 2R, well spaced K guards to W	
Ferguson of Balquhidder	B	K	G	G	K	R edge to B
Leslie, Hunting	B	K	G	R	K	W edge to G
Logan (MacLennan)	B	K	G	5R	RKYKR	
MacCallum	B	K	G	K	AK near each edge; A outermost	
MacEwen	B	K	G	2K	R/Y, K guards	
MacLaren	B	K	G	—	Y, 2R, well spaced, K guards to Y	
MacLeod of Harris	B	K	G	Y, K guards	R, K guards	
MacNeil	B	K	G	W	Y, K guards	
Malcolm	B	K	G	2R	KYKAK	
Ogilvie, Hunting	B	K	G	—	R, 4K	Y edge to B
Rose, Hunting	B	K	G	R	K, W guards	
Sinclair, Hunting*	B	K	G	R	2R	W edge to B
Dunbar*	R	K	G	2K	R	
Ruthven*	R	B	G	2G	W	

Three-colour checks with simple overcheck, and strip

As is now usual, * indicates Vest.Scot. designs. The composite line KYKAK in Malcolm always comes in the same order, thus making the tartan a non-reversing one.

The MacDonald Group

The dark tartan of the Clan Donald takes the three-colour check a stage further, adding to the basic design a recognition feature that is common to the branches of the Clan and which, at the same time outlines a motif that is used in other MacDonald setts. Reference to the colour strip (No. 20, on page 84) will help in the interpretation of the sketches of the variations.

The MacDonald motif in the parent tartans is in negative form, shown by the ground showing through between the lines of the pattern. In positive form, as a wide line with a narrow one each side, it is an old device of the tartan weaver, and appears in many tartans, not all necessarily being MacDonald or related to that Clan.

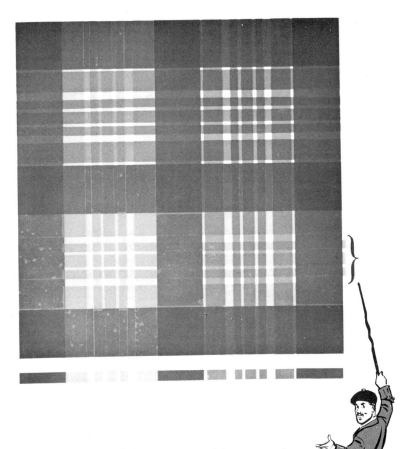

In the tartans of the MacDonald group, the ground showing through makes three lines, like this. Colour strips 20, 21, 22, 23 and 24 on page 84 show this quite clearly. Have a look. The black and white strips over the page show them as well.

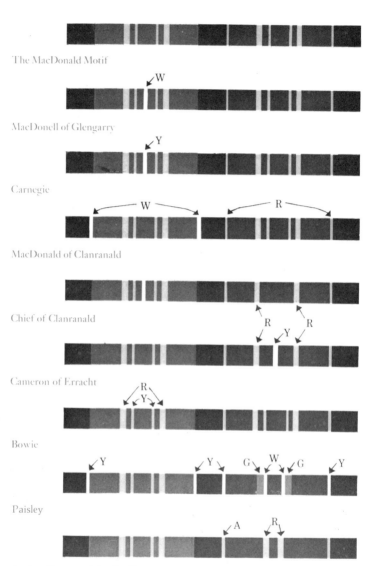

The MacDonald Motif

MacDonell of Glengarry

Carnegie

MacDonald of Clanranald

Chief of Clanranald

Cameron of Erracht

Bowie

Paisley

Ancient Stewart of Appin, Hunting

The Black Watch Group

One of the best known — and certainly one of the most popular — tartans is that of the Royal Highland Regiment, the **Black Watch.** It is popular with tartan designers as well as with the public at large, for nothing could be easier than to juggle with an established pattern to produce a new one.

Many stories are told of the origin of the tartan, none of which can be proved conclusively. What we certainly know is that the 42nd has used at least three tartans in its time, one being a plain blue, black and green check over-checked with red on each of the colours (i.e., the blue and the green) and the third a bandsmen's plaid in which the black of the ordinary sett was made red. The present sett has been called the 'Government tartan', because it is the basis of all the military tartans (except **Cameron of Erracht** which was designed for the 79th Cameron Highlanders when the regiment was raised). It has been dubbed the 'Universal tartan' for similar reasons. Repetition lends authority to statements of doubtful worth, and the name 'Universal' came to carry with it the suggestion that the tartan is the correct one for general use by those having no tartan of their own, an idea equivalent to proposing that R.A.F. 'wings' should be used to decorate a sports jacket. In the earliest records of the pattern it is noted as '42nd Pattern', no more and no less.

Another popular misconception that can be disposed of is that the Regiment derived its nickname from its dark tartan and was called Black Watch to distinguish it from the 'Red Soldiers'. The 42nd originated in the Independent Companies of the Highland Watch raised in 1729 with the special object of dealing with the practise of 'Black Mail', a 'protection racket' operated by some of the less law-abiding Clans. In this context, 'Mail' meant tax, and 'Black' illegal, and the name of the regiment comes from its duty as a Watch, or police force, operating against the Black Mailers.

Tartans based upon 42nd Pattern fall into three groups:

Group 1. The basic tartan with one or more coloured overchecks;

Group 2. The basic tartan with colours changed; and

Group 3. Tartans wrapped round the——— ———motif.

Group 1. Tartans based directly upon Black Watch.

$$\left[\ \blacksquare = K \quad \text{(dotted)} = B \quad \text{(hatched)} = G\ \right]$$

Name	1	2	3	Comments
Arbuthnott	—	B, 2W	2K	
Baillie of Polkemett	—	3W	2K	
Campbell of Argyll	—	W/Y K guards	—	
Campbell of Breadalbane (Fencibles)	—	—	2K	Y edges to G
Cheape	—	A	2K	
Dyce	—	YKY	W	
Farquharson	R	Y	R, K guards	
Forbes	—	W, K guards	2K	
Gordon (92nd Regiment)	—	Y	2K	
„ (Vest.Scot.)	—	3Y	2K	
Lamont	—	W	2K	
Mackenzie (Seaforth)	—	W, K guards	R, K guards	
MacKinlay	—	R, K guards	2K	
Murray of Athol	—	R	R, K guards	
Polaris	—	YKBKY	2K	
Robertson of Kindeace		R, K guards	W, K guards	
Sutherland	All as Black Watch but in lighter colours			

Group 2. This small group comprises only three tartans apart from the parent, but all provide excellent examples of the way in which a tartan can be changed out of all recognition without interfering with the pattern. It will be as well to deal with the biggest change first, and this is the **MacNab** tartan, a striking design in scarlet, crimson and green; crimson replaces the black of the Black Watch, green replaces the blue and scarlet replaces the green.

In examining tartans, a set of photographic colour filters in red, blue and green is a most useful accessory, and its usefulness can be demonstrated very clearly here. Look at Black Watch through a deep blue filter and then at MacNab through a red one and you will be in no doubt as to the basis of MacNab.

MacLachlan goes less far. Blue is changed to red and green to blue; what was a black line on green becomes a green one on blue.

Finally, one of several **Urquhart** tartans reverses the blue and the green and puts a red line on the (now) blue. Colour strips of Black Watch, MacNab, MacLachlan and Urquhart have been included on page 83 (strips 13, 14, 15 and 16) to show the relationship of these.

Group 3. With a ready-made motif suitable for dumping in the middle of almost any kind of pattern, we need not be surprised that Group 3 contains many tartans that first saw the light of day in the 'Vestiarium Scoticum'.

Group 3. Tartans based on the Black Watch motif.

Name	▨	▓	▒	☐	▥
Abercrombie	B	K	G	—	2W
Armstrong*	B	K	G	R	2K
Chisholm, Hunting*	G	B	R	R	2W
Cranstoun*	DG	B	LG	—	R
Kerr*	G	K	R	—	3K
Lindsay*	G	B	C	—	2B
MacDonald, Lord of the Isles*	G	K	B	W	R
MacRae, Hunting	G	K, but line nearest K bar is C	B or P	—	W, K edges
Stewart of Athol*	G	K	R	—	2K
Stewart of Bute*	G	K	R	wide R	W
Sutherland*	B	K	G	3R	2W
Urquhart	B	K	G	R	K
,, *	B	K	G	2W	2K, R central

55

A distinct offshoot of the plain three-colour check employs the same colours but adds a green and a black section to each repeat, so that the base pattern reads B-K-G-K-G-K instead of B-K-G-K. Upon this foundation, **Campbell of Breadalbane** has a yellow overcheck on green, **Graham of Montrose** a white one and **MacCallum** a red one. All have a single black overcheck on blue. **MacNeil of Colonsay** differs from Graham of Montrose only in having a blue bar between the green stripes instead of black.

Graham of Montrose and Campbell of Breadalbane both appeared in the Wilson 1819 Key Pattern Book, but under the designations of 'No 64' and 'No 2/64'; at that time No 64 was called 'Abercrombie pattern' (not to be confused with modern **Abercrombie** as shown on page 55), and its cousin had no name, which shows how tartans get around!

The MacDuff Group

The red **MacDuff** tartan fathers a small clan of setts whose chief distinguishing feature is a red square with a blue border; the blue may be light or dark and, in 'modern' colours is frequently a rather sickly shade of Royal blue. Still, one of the group is **Royal Stuart,** so we must swallow our feelings and try to believe that someone felt this to be appropriate.

It is always tempting to regard the simplest of a group of patterns as the oldest, but we can rarely if ever have any firm proof of age. In this case **MacDuff** has been chosen as the founder of the group because it appears, entirely upon inspection, to have more of the basic features of the design than either **Sinclair** or **Menzies.**

With the exception of Sinclair, all the tartans shown in the shaded 'colour' strips on page 59 appeared in Wilson's 1819 pattern book, a work that is so important to the practical student that we have to remind ourselves frequently that its compilers were not the only practitioners of what was even then a competitive business, lest we fall into the trap of believing everything that it tells us. This would be fatal to real research.

What Wilsons, or anyone else for that matter, do not tell us in most cases is whence these tartans came. Our **MacPherson** was 'No 43, or Kidd Sett, or Caledonia Pattern' to them, and our **Caledonia** was simply 'No 155'. King Charles II is said to have worn tartan shoulder knots at his wedding, and to some authorities it is 'obvious' that these were of the Royal Stuart pattern, but 'obvious' is a dangerous word which lends seeming rectitude to the most dubious

statements. Among the many pieces of tartan said to have been worn by Prince Charles Edward at the Battle of Culloden, there are several examples of the tartan known by his name and called by Wilsons 'Prince Charles Stuart's Tartan'; while we do not need to argue here the point that His Royal Highness could hardly have galloped off the field if he had been wearing all the plaids that claim this distinction, we can point out that the difference between this tartan and Royal Stuart is merely a matter of a shift of emphasis from one red end of the sett to the other, and that **Prince Charles Edward** may perhaps be the basis of the other design.

How Wilsons' 'No 3 Caledonia' disappeared from sight and became replaced first by 'No 43' and then by 'No 155' is a story that must remain unanswered, although it is likely that an important factor was the confusion that always seems to have arisen when the Clan Chiefs took a hand in reviving their Clan tartans. We will recall that tartan was proscribed for thirty-five years, so it is not surprising that some doubts should have been entertained over which was the correct pattern—and some wrong choices made as a result.

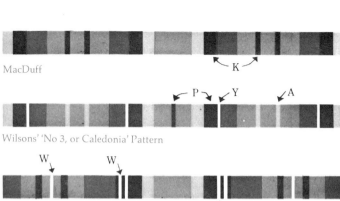

MacDuff

Wilsons' 'No 3, or Caledonia' Pattern

Prince Charles Edward

Royal Stuart

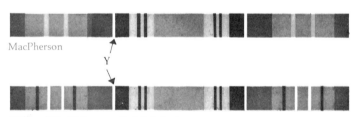

MacPherson

Wilsons' 'No 155', now called Caledonia

Sinclair, Dress

Menzies

Non-reversing Patterns

All the tartans so far discussed have, ostensibly at any rate, been of the type which follows the rule that the pattern repeats regularly by reversing about its two axes and is the same in both directions of the cloth. In fact, any tartan in which a line occurs which alternates in colour in each half sett is, strictly speaking, non-reversing, although it is only this feature that makes it so. Examination of **Black Watch** and **Campbell of Argyll** will show how this comes about, and a worthwhile exercise is to go through the preceding tables and sort out the patterns of this kind.

In earlier days, when tartan was less regimented than it is now, it was not uncommon for it to be made with the warp and weft patterns differing, and some surviving specimens from the Hebrides show some very subtle distinctions of this kind. Nowadays, this is rare and most unlikely to be seen in the street, so no more need be said.

A pattern that does appear in the street is the very, almost too, familiar **Buchanan.** Somehow it nearly always manages to look as if it is printed on flannel instead of woven in wool. In his book 'The Scottish Gael', published in 1831,

James Logan recorded a Buchanan tartan of red and green squares separated by groups of light-blue and yellow lines; this was a regular reversing pattern of an exceptionally neat appearance. In the same book, he recorded that the MacMillans wore the same tartan as the Buchanans. Later, Logan furnished information to the artist R. R. McIan, who produced the pictures for a book 'The Clans of the Scottish Highlands'. McIan no doubt did his best, but the result showed a clearly non-reversing tartan under the name **Buchanan** and another somewhat similar under the name **MacMillan.** The latter is now marketed under the name of **Ancient MacMillan,** while the original Logan version of Buchanan shows some signs of superseding the McIan version.

For purposes of comparison, colour strips of the two Buchanan tartans are shown on page 85 under the numbers 25 for the non-reversing sett and 26 for the reversing one; Ancient MacMillan differs most obviously from the non-reversing Buchanan in omitting all the blue in favour of green and in leaving out the white over-check on the red ground, which is usually a rather 'plummy' shade.

Hunting and Dress Tartans

The colours produced by the old natural dyes were bright but soft, and the tartans dyed with them were characterised by the way the colours blended without clashing. But the Victorians were great 'improvers', and when they got hold of the first synthetic dyestuffs the process of adding strength and brilliance began. It has been said, and not without some justification that discussion of tartans generates more heat than light, but one sometimes gets the impression that Victorian tartans were designed to shine in the dark, and to show their wearers the way home on the darkest nights!

Victorian times also saw the heyday of Highland sport. The object of much of this being to shoot a stag rather than stun it, it became necessary to have hunting tartans of somewhat less striking appearance than those in everyday use. Leaning heavily upon an early reporter, George Buchanan, who referred to dark brown clothing worn for purposes of camouflage, the result almost always turned out to be the ordinary red Clan tartan made in brown or green. The list is too long to go into in detail, but **Fraser, Scott** and **MacKinnon** may be mentioned among those having a brown ground; **Mackintosh** and **Shaw** have the main red ground changed to green and **Cameron** changes the main ground to blue and gives the yellow line green edges. Most of the hunting variations have some such minor alteration as this last— Fraser, for example, alternating a red overcheck with the white—but such changes **are** minor and of little overall significance for recognition purposes.

By extension of an idea, the term 'hunting' has become generally applied to the darker tartan when a Clan has a red one as well; what is now called **Hunting MacLean** was just 'MacLean' in the 'Vestiarium Scoticum'. An exception to the rule is **Hunting Stewart** which, although the first tartan to which the description was applied, now appears to be neither Hunting nor Stewart in its origin, but a tartan for general use since its inception, although it did not become popular until some twenty years after that. As first recorded by Wilsons in 1819 it differed slightly and to its benefit from the version sold nowadays and is also unique in being the only non-reversing proper tartan in the list at that time. Colour strips of the two varieties are included at the end of the book (Nos 6 and 7 on page 82).

Victorian times also brought a great proliferation of

tartans for every purpose, some people even claiming funeral setts. Few, however, went further than to have 'Dress' tartans, compounded in much the same way as Hunting setts but by weaving on a white ground instead of a dark one. The whole basis of these tartans lies in a mistranslation of the word Dress, which is taken to mean men's formal attire instead of the outermost article of women's everyday wear. Although the pattern was never associated with a Clan, the material used for the women's plaids in olden times was nearly always woven on a white ground and the modern Dress tartans are developed from this, having now achieved Clan status. Dress tartans are therefore strictly for the ladies!

Of course, those lucky enough to have dark Clan tartans did not need to manufacture Hunting setts and those with ready-to-hand bright ones were able to keep out of the Dress tartan business. But there are plenty of both to be seen for all that.

The Others

The register of tartans, which the Scottish Tartans Society has compiled over the past ten years now comprises about 1200 record cards, each of which carries the colour strip, thread count and other basic data of one sett. Fortunately, this is not to say that the tartan-spotter is in imminent danger of running into any one of 1200 different tartans, for several setts occupy up to five cards each and there are many patterns that are tartans in name only, being woven as small check patterns in tartan cloth. A very large proportion of those recorded have never attained the dignity of having a name. A cautious guess suggests that when all these have been removed, there remain somewhere in the region of six hundred tartans that are actually in use somewhere at some times. But even this is a tidy few, and not by any means all of them can be fitted easily into the simple design classifications that we have used.

Just like any other good jigsaw puzzle, tartans should not be forced to fit the rest of the picture. To do this would be to jeopardise the whole of the rest of the puzzle, and it is much better to treat the 'rogue' patterns on their merits as they crop up.

Some of the rogue patterns are simple, like the dark-blue **Montgomerie** with its black bars bearing alternately pairs of red and pale green lines, or **Elliot,** another blue tartan —this time with pairs of maroon bars with a red line between. But with most of these rogues it is their very complication that prevents them from forming a group. Although we may sometimes come across one of these which carries its own identifying mark, such as the almost unique pale blue background that goes with the **Anderson** tartan, the best way of dealing with them is to make our own colour strips and so begin to keep a proper record of the tartans that we have spotted. This is not by any means a difficult task, but it is first necessary to learn how to examine a tartan and record the data that we discover.

COLLECTING, EXAMINING AND RECORDING TARTANS

For the purposes of this exercise we may assume a tartan without complications, that is one that is woven in twill weave and in which the pattern reverses properly about the pivotal lines and is the same in both directions of the cloth. For practice in taking thread counts a piece of fairly heavy weight worsted cloth in 'ancient' colours is best, as the threads will show up more clearly and the colours will be easier to distinguish.

The first step is to decide upon the pivots; this is not difficult to do, for the pattern will repeat exactly on each side of any pivot, but some care is necessary even in this elementary operation, for it is not all that difficult to find a false pivot and so produce a new tartan that will puzzle posterity! Having found the pivots, the next job is to list the colours of each stripe in order from one pivot to the next, using the colour symbols given on the fold-out flap of the back cover. These symbols are those used by the Scottish Tartans Society and have the great merits of being simple and unambiguous. Some authorities have used Bk for Black and Bl for Blue, which quickly results in confusion. The use of heraldic names for the colours has also been tried with dire results, for not only is the range of colours quite inadequate for the purpose, necessitating importation of extra colours, but such facts as G meaning Gules (which is red) and A being both Azure and Argent have left us some problems. The symbols on the flap are the clearest yet devised.

Having found the pivots and listed the colours, underline the pivots to pick them out from the other elements of the pattern. The beginning and end of a non-reversing count are marked with rows of dots leading up to the beginning and away from the end.

With all the preparatory work done, we now come to the business of actually counting the threads of each stripe. The twill weave is of great help to us in this, for its 'over two, under two' construction makes it, for the purpose of counting threads, only half as fine as it really is. The best place to start counting is at the junction of two colours, where the colour to be counted appears solid and the next one a blend made up of diagonal ribs of the first and second colours. All that has to be done is to count the total number of ribs—that is, both colours—and multiply the result by two. Some care is still necessary, but it is now relative; the world will not come to an end if you are two threads out in a hundred, but to count two or six where the right answer is four is a major error. Take your count at right angles to the selvedge if you can determine this, because this will be the warp count which is set up in the loom and cannot vary as the weaving goes on. The weft, particularly in old pieces, can be subject to the weaver keeping count of the number of times he throws the shuttle and so is more subject to error.

You now have a thread count, but for good measure you should note any other characteristics of the cloth, take a measurement of the centre-to-centre size of the pattern and measure the number of threads per inch.

The next thing to do, and a most necessary precaution, is to check everything thoroughly:

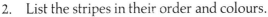

1. Locate the pivots.
2. List the stripes in their order and colours.
3. Mark the pivots, if it is a reversing count, or the ends if it is a non-reversing count.
4. Take the count of each stripe.
5. Measure the size of the sett, or half sett.
6. Make an independent calculation of the number of threads per inch.
7. Add anything else you think you should add.
8. CHECK EVERYTHING.

What you now have will look something like this, which is the actual thread count taken from a piece of **Clanchattan** tartan: —

R	K	W	G	W	Y	R	K	R	Y	W	A	K	R	Y	W
104	4	2	26	2	6	6	2	6	6	2	26	8	8	10	4

Half sett $= 4\frac{1}{4}''$ 40 threads per inch

(MacFarlane, by the way, is an identical scheme, with the light blue of **Clanchattan** changed to purple, yellow to white and white to green.)

In normal practice, the colour strip is drawn along the top edge of the filing record card which carries the rest of the data on its face. It must be admitted that a modicum of skill is required for the successful production of colour strips, but it is not all that difficult a matter.

It is usual to use 8″ x 5″ cards, and the strip is set out in the proportions of the count to a scale at which the half-sett of a reversing pattern, or the entire repeat of a non-reversing one, will occupy about five inches, one-and-a-half inches at each end being used to show the continuation of the repeat in both directions. The colours are then filled in with poster colour or fibre-tipped pen to make a strip about a quarter of an inch wide. **There are no standard colours for tartans,** and for this reason it is preferable that the colours used for strips should be diagrammatic unless special conditions dictate otherwise.

When using poster colours, a ruling pen of the old-fashioned kind that has two adjustable blades will be found helpful in making neat edges to the bands of colour.

The final operation in producing a well turned-out record card is to put a small cross under each pivot, write the card up and index it.

'Sindex', the system of indexing devised by Donald C. Stewart for the Scottish Tartans Society, is simple and effective. Taking a typical reversing pattern as an example, 'Sindex' will give it a coding which consists in its basic form of two three-letter groups which indicate the first three colours inwards from each end of the half-sett, using the symbols with which we are already familiar. For this purpose we do not worry about shades of colour other than light blue; apart from this, all blues are B, all reds R and so on . The two groups are separated by a colon and placed in alphabetical order. Thus the **Clanchattan** tartan of our example is designated RKW: WYR, and not WYR:RKW. If there are fewer than six stripes in a tartan, the second code group is cut back as far as one letter, after which the first group is reduced; five stripes produce a coding as ABC:DE, four as ABC:D and three as AB:C. Non-reversing patterns have only a single group of letters, beginning with the colour symbol that comes first alphabetically and going in the direction of that which comes alphabetically next. Since a non-reversing pattern has no pivot, the sett can start anywhere in its length. For example, non-reversing tartan having a light-blue stripe will always start with . . .A. Generally speaking, the three-letter symbols are adequate for most users of 'Sindex', but in the full-size version it is sometimes necessary to add letters to the second group to differentiate between two tartans whose three-letter groups are the same.

There is, in fact, a lot more to 'Sindex' than that, but this will be enough to be going on with.

FURTHER READING

By now, you will either be defeated or bitten by the tartan bug; if the former, we can only say "Try again!" but for the latter complaint the Scottish Tartans Society can offer the means of making the affliction easier to bear (the disease itself is incurable). The Society is based at Broughty Castle, Broughty Ferry, Dundee, and in return for a very modest Membership subscription will advise, assist and encourage the student of tartan to the best of the combined abilities of its Members.

This book has set out to do no more than raise interest by showing that tartan is more than just a lot of pretty patterns backed up by 'What is my Tartan' lists. Where he goes from there is the reader's own business. 'Tartanology' is not yet a subject which cannot be attempted without a University education. The rules of the game have scarcely yet been formulated and can be summed up as being 'To seek tartan in places where you do not expect to find it and, having found it there, to catalogue it with the utmost care'. After a bit of this, one's own abilities come to the fore and some specialization tends to set in. We hope that by then there will be some more books about it to take you a bit further.

'The Setts of the Scottish Tartans' by Donald C. Stewart, Oliver & Boyd 1950) is an unquestionable choice for the student seriously interested in tartans. As the first modern detailed work about tartans, it laid the foundations of what amounts to a new science, compounded of archaeology, detection, and practical research.

A ready-to-hand collection of tartans for examination is a necessity and is provided in book form by Robert Bain's 'Clans and Tartans of Scotland' (Collins) and Sir Thomas Innes of Learney's 'Tartans of the Clans and Families of Scotland'. Historical books of this class, well worth study, are 'The Clans of the Highlands of Scotland' by Thomas Smibert, published in 1850, 'Authenticated Tartans of the Clans and Families of Scotland' by William and Andrew Smith, published at Mauchline also in 1850, and 'Tartans of the Clans of Scotland' by James Grant, published in 1886. In a class by itself is 'Old and Rare Scottish Tartans' the product of much careful research by the author, D. W. Stewart, and illustrated by woven silk 'colour plates'.

The study of tartans is a highly practical affair, and the answer to many questions lies in ones own ability to ask, and to answer, the question 'What would I do in a case like that?' This makes learning to weave almost obligatory, at least up to the standard of being able to make small specimens. 'Handweaving' by Eve Cherry, in the 'Teach Yourself' series is a fully adequate book for the purpose, and includes instructions for making a small table loom.

TARTAN INDEX

THREAD COUNTS

There being at the time of writing no readily available source-book of tartan patterns, we have thought it proper to include some thread counts. They are not only intended for the benefit of our weaver-readers, for they will also be useful to non-weavers who want to have a go at making some colour strips, and have already been of the greatest help to the author in his attempts to squeeze still more tartans into a very limited space.

The method of presenting the counts is not universal, but follows the form used for the Scottish Tartans Society's record cards, i.e. a row of dots leading up to the count indicates a non-reversing count and an underline to the end colours a reversing one; in the latter case, the pivot stripes are quoted their full width.

For practical weaving purposes, a count will almost always have to be adjusted to take into account the gauge of the yarn and the size of sett required. This is where the tartan-weaver's art comes in, and here we must leave the subject.

1. Anderson

R	A	R	K	R	A	K	W	K	Y	K	Y	K	R	B	R
6	12	2	4	2	36	6	6	6	2	2	2	8	2	8	6

G	R	G	R
12	4	12	8

2. Black Watch

B	K	B	K	B	K	G	K	G	K	B	K	B
32	6	6	6	6	32	30	6	30	32	30	6	6

3. Buchanan (see colour strip 26, page 85)

A	G	K	A	K	Y	K	Y	K	A	K	R	W
4	32	2	4	2	8	2	8	2	4	2	32	4

4. Cameron of Lochiel

R	G	R	B*	W	B*	R	B	R	*or K
12	6	12	2	4	2	4	16	8	

5. Cumming

K	R	G	R	K	B	R	G	R	K	R	B+ K alt. K+ B
2	2	16	2	12	2	12	12	2	16	2	2

6. Drummond of Perth

R	W	P	Y	G	R	P	A	W
72	2	6	2	32	16	6	4	2

7. Fraser of Lovat (see colour strip 2, page 82)

B	R	B	R	G	R	W	R	G	B	R	B
32	2	2	2	24	32	4	32	24	24	2	2

8. Hay (Leith)

K	R	Y	K	R	G	R	Y	R	G	W	K	R	P	R	Y
6	2	2	4	32	4	2	2	4	30	2	30	2	30	4	2

R	P	R	K	Y	R	K
2	4	32	4	2	2	6

9. MacAlister

R	LG	DG	R	A	R	W	R	A	R	DG	R	W	R	A	R
16	2	4	4	2	2	2	2	2	4	6	2	2	12	2	2

DG	R	A	R	A	R	DG	R	A	R	W	R	B	R	W	R
24	2	2	32	2	2	24	2	2	12	2	2	8	2	2	4

DG	LG	R	LG	DG	R	W	R	B	R	W	R
6	2	4	2	6	6	2	2	4	2	2	16

10. MacBain

G	W	R	C	G	C	R	W	K	G	K	W	A	K	W	K
20	4	10	10	4	10	10	4	4	24	4	4	10	4	4	4

A	W	R
10	4	120

11. MacDonald (see colour strip 20, page 84)

B	R	B	R	B	R	K	G	R	G	R	G
26	4	4	8	38	4	38	38	8	4	4	26

12. MacDonell of Keppoch (see colour strip 12, page 83)

G	R	B	R	B	R	G	R	B
4	4	2	48	12	6	24	8	2

13. MacDougal

A	R	Pink	C	R	P	R	G	R	G	C	Pk	R	Pk	C
2	6	4	6	52	4	4	20	20	20	6	4	4	4	6

P	R	G	R	G	R	Pk	C	A
20	8	4	8	54	4	4	8	2

14. MacDuff (see colour strip 17, page 84)

R	K	R	G	K	A	R
8	2	8	12	8	6	16

15. MacKinnon

W	R	G	P	R	G	R	P	G	R	G	Pink	R	W
4	8	6	6	18	48	6	10	6	50	18	6	8	4

16. Mackintosh (see colour strip 8, page 82)

B	R	G	R	B	R
2	6	22	4	10	44

17. MacLaine of Lochbuie

R	G	A	Y
64	16	8	2

18. MacLean of Duart

K	R	A	R	G	K	W	K	Y	K	A	B
2	4	2	24	16	2	2	2	2	6	2	8

19. MacMillan, Dress
<u>R</u> Y R Y R Y R Y <u>R</u>
2 16 4 16 6 4 24 2 6

20. Menzies
<u>R</u> W R W R W R <u>W</u>   Dress
<u>G</u> R G R G R G <u>R</u>   Hunting
<u>K</u> W K W K W K <u>W</u>   Clan
72 8 6 8 12 4 2 24

21. Ogilvie
<u>W</u> A Y K R W R W R K Y A R <u>A</u>
2 8 2 2 12 2 8 2 12 2 2 8 2 8

22. Rae (see colour strip 3, page 82)
<u>P</u> G P G P G P G P G P G P G P G
54 12 54 56 10 14 10 56 62 12 62 56 4 4 8 4
P G P G P G P G P G <u>P</u>
4 56 4 4 8 4 4 56 54 12 4

23. Robertson
<u>R</u> G R P R G R P R P R G <u>R</u>
6 6 70 6 6 70 6 70 6 6 70 6 6

24. Scott
<u>G</u> R K R G R G W G <u>R</u>
8 6 2 56 28 8 8 6 8 8

25. Thomson (MacTavish)
<u>A</u> R B A K <u>A</u>
4 24 4 12 12 2

COLOUR STRIPS

With one exception, the colour strips have been chosen for the purpose of illustrating points made in the text. (In order to do this adequately it has sometimes been necessary to make some slight distortions of the proportions; this is never serious, but the thirster after patterns should beware of scaling up the strips and using the result as a weaving scale. Small errors in registration while printing can result in the formation of thin black or white lines where colours join, and this is another reason for regarding the strips as illustrations rather than accurate sources of reference.)

The exception mentioned above is the second Fraser strip (Fraser of Lovat), which represents a tartan claimed to have been worn by a member of the Clan at Culloden.

One theory that has been put forward concerning the origins of the tartans that made their first known appearance in the 'Vestiarium Scoticum' is that John Sobieski first wrote descriptions from tartans which were in existence at the time of the discovery of the manuscripts and that Charles subsequently drew the pictures from these descriptions. The description in the Cromarty manuscript reads 'Fryzzel heth four stryppis upon ain scarlatt (fie)ld quhairoff the outerward be of greine and the (inner)ward of blewe and upone the scarlatte sette ain sprainge of quhite of saxteine threidis.' The precise value of such a description will doubtless be apparent to the reader without further explanation!

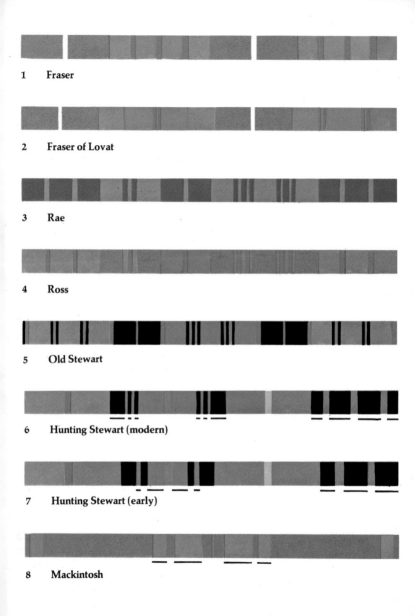

1 Fraser

2 Fraser of Lovat

3 Rae

4 Ross

5 Old Stewart

6 Hunting Stewart (modern)

7 Hunting Stewart (early)

8 Mackintosh

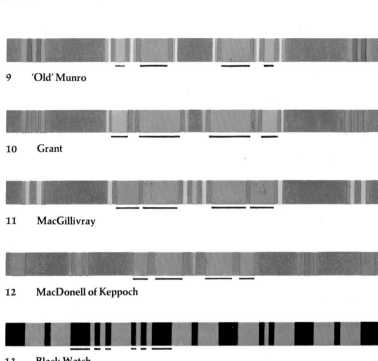

9   'Old' Munro

10   Grant

11   MacGillivray

12   MacDonell of Keppoch

13   Black Watch

14   MacNab

15   MacLachlan (MacLauchlan)

16   Urquhart

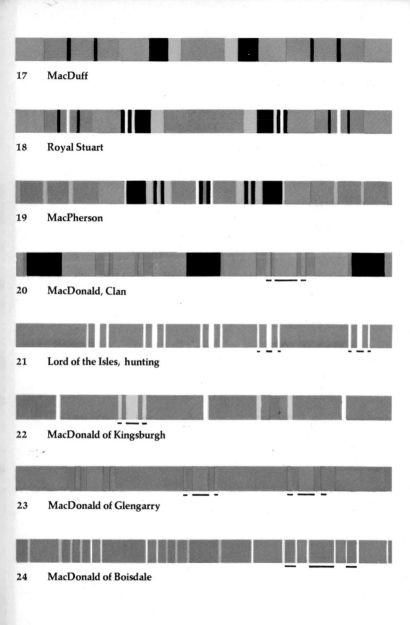

17 MacDuff

18 Royal Stuart

19 MacPherson

20 MacDonald, Clan

21 Lord of the Isles, hunting

22 MacDonald of Kingsburgh

23 MacDonald of Glengarry

24 MacDonald of Boisdale